Y0-CDP-860

Rocks

Claudia Martin

Quarto is the authority on a wide range of topics.

Quarto educates, entertains and enriches the lives of our readers—enthusiasts and lovers of hands-on living.

www.quartoknows.com

Editor: Clare Hibbert
Designer: Dave Ball

© 2017 Quarto Publishing plc
First Published in 2017 by QEB Publishing,
an imprint of The Quarto Group.
6 Orchard Road,
Suite 100,
Lake Forest, CA 92630
T: +1 949 380 7510
F: +1 949 380 7575
www.QuartoKnows.com

All rights reserved. No part of this publication may be reproduced, stored in a retrieval system, or transmitted in any form or by any means, electronic, mechanical, photocopying, recording, or otherwise, without the prior permission of the publisher, nor be otherwise circulated in any form of binding or cover other than that in which it is published and without a similar condition being imposed on the subsequent purchaser.

A CIP record for this book is available from the Library of Congress.

ISBN 978-1-68297-364-6

Manufactured in Shenzhen, China RD102017
9 8 7 6 5 4 3 2 1

MIX
Paper from
responsible sources
FSC® C101537
FSC
www.fsc.org

Contents

What is **Rock?**

Underneath cities, grass, and oceans, the Earth's surface is made of rock. Rock is solid, but it can be hard or soft, crumbly or flaky.

basalt

flint

clay

marble

chalk

MADE OF MINERALS

There are lots of different sorts of rocks. Rocks look and feel different from each other because they are mixtures of different minerals. Minerals are solids that form in the ground or in water.

These cliffs in Yosemite National Park are made of the rock granite. ▶

ALL MIXED UP

The dark speckles in granite are made from minerals such as mica. The lighter areas are made from the minerals quartz and feldspar.

▲ You can see large grains of minerals in granite.

Earth's plates

The Earth's surface is split into giant plates of rock, like jigsaw pieces.

▼ When Earth's plates rub against each other, they cause earthquakes.

How Rocks are Made

There are three kinds of rock: igneous, sedimentary, and metamorphic. Each kind is made in a different way.

IGNEOUS ROCKS

Beneath Earth's surface is hot, runny rock called magma. When magma cools, it hardens into igneous rocks such as basalt, granite, and pumice.

Japan's Mount Fuji is made mostly of basalt, which is cooled lava.

Sometimes magma spews out of a volcano as lava.

SEDIMENTARY ROCKS

When mud, sand, or dead plants and animals are pressed together for thousands of years, they harden into sedimentary rocks. Limestone, chalk, and clay are sedimentary rocks.

These chalk cliffs are made of millions of shells that piled up on the sea floor. ▼

METAMORPHIC ROCKS

Movements inside the Earth can press and heat rocks. They change into a new type of rock: metamorphic rock. Marble, slate, and hornfels are metamorphic rocks.

This marble was made when limestone was pressed and heated.

That's old!

Sedimentary rock in Australia's Jack Hills contains the oldest materials on Earth—minerals that are 4.4 billion years old!

▼ A satellite image of the Jack Hills

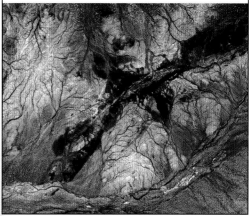

Is Rock **Useful?**

Rock was one of the earliest materials that humans put to practical use. Today, we use it for many different purposes.

The White Tower, in the Tower of London, was built from limestone. ▼

STRONG ROCK

We use strong rocks such as granite, marble, and limestone to build homes, offices, and monuments. Tough, waterproof slate tiles our roofs.

SOFT ROCK

Potters mold soft clay into bowls and plates. They fire (bake) the clay till it is hard.

◄ These dishes are about to be fired.

BURNABLE ROCK

The sedimentary rock coal is made from plants and animals that lived millions of years ago. It is used as a fuel because it burns easily.

▲ Burning coals give out heat and light.

These tools, found in Tanzania, are from 1.8 million years ago. ▶

The Stone Age

The earliest stone tools are more than three million years old.

What is **Sand?**

Sand is tiny bits of broken rock. Its color depends on the rocks it came from.

FROM ROCK TO SAND...

Sand is made when wind, waves, rain, or rivers rub away at rocks. This is called erosion.

▼ The Sahara Desert's sand is made mostly of the mineral quartz, worn from common rocks such as granite.

SANDY BEACHES

At the seaside, the waves make sand by eroding cliffs, shells, and coral reefs.

▼ Black sand, made from basalt, is found on beaches near a volcano.

FROM SAND TO ROCK...

If sand is buried and pressed for thousands of years, it turns into rock called sandstone. Movements in the ground can push the sandstone to the surface.

These sandstone towers, or buttes, are in Monument Valley, Arizona. ▼

Brain-boggling beaches

The Earth's beaches contain five sextillion grains of sand—that is 5 with 21 zeroes!

All About
Caves

Underground caves are made by rainwater. The water soaks into the ground and then wears away the rock.

GOING, GOING, GONE!

Caves often form in limestone, because this rock dissolves in rainwater—tiny bits of it mix with the water and are carried away. As rainwater trickles through limestone, any cracks slowly widen into caves.

▲ Over time, underground rivers wear away a wide path through limestone.

STALACTITES

As rainwater travels through limestone, it collects minerals from the rock. When water drips from the cave's roof, it leaves behind minerals that form dangling stalactites.

◀ A stalactite hangs down from the ceiling of the cave.

A stalagmite points up from the ground in the cave. ▶

STALAGMITES

In pools of water on a cave floor, minerals can build into towering stalagmites.

Record breaker

The world's longest cave is Mammoth Cave in Kentucky. It has 405 miles (652 km) of passageways.

▼ The Devil's Pit, a limestone cave near Pottenstein in Germany

How Minerals
Grow

Some minerals grow in hot rocks or magma.
Other amazing minerals grow in water.

STARTING TO GROW

Minerals are made of elements,
the basic building materials for
everything on Earth. When tiny
atoms of elements link together,
minerals grow. They make
regular shapes called crystals.

The mineral pyrite forms
cube-shaped crystals.

The mineral aragonite
forms "flower"-shaped
crystals.

GROWING IN THE GROUND

Long crystals of epidote grow in hot rocks. This mineral is made from the elements calcium, aluminum, iron, silicon, and oxygen.

Epidote crystals are usually green. ▶

GROWING IN THE WATER

The mineral gypsum contains the elements calcium, sulfur, oxygen, and hydrogen. It grows as water evaporates, leaving behind the tiny solid elements that were floating in it.

Common mineral

Quartz is one of the most common minerals on planet Earth. It is made from the elements silicon and oxygen.

◀ This gypsum formed on a cave floor.

All About
Metals

Metals are minerals that are found in rocks. They are strong, shiny, and very useful.

MINING FOR METAL

Miners dig or blast into the ground to find metals. Sometimes, they find pure nuggets or flakes of metal. Usually metals are mixed with other minerals.

An underground gold mine

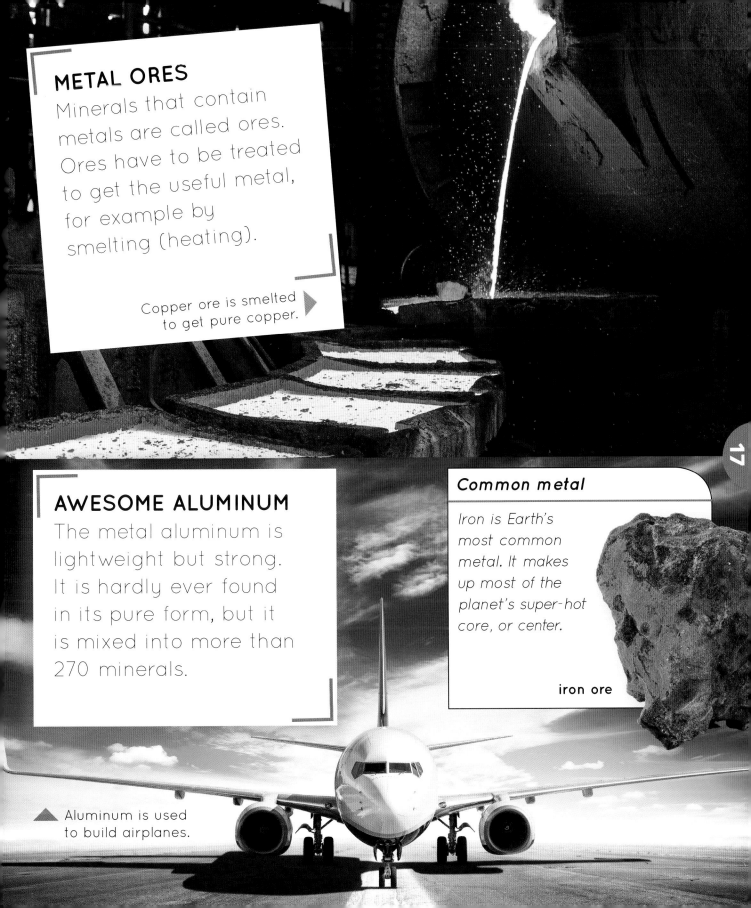

METAL ORES

Minerals that contain metals are called ores. Ores have to be treated to get the useful metal, for example by smelting (heating).

Copper ore is smelted to get pure copper. ▶

AWESOME ALUMINUM

The metal aluminum is lightweight but strong. It is hardly ever found in its pure form, but it is mixed into more than 270 minerals.

Common metal

Iron is Earth's most common metal. It makes up most of the planet's super-hot core, or center.

iron ore

▲ Aluminum is used to build airplanes.

Why are Gems Precious?

Gems are minerals or rocks that are so hard, colorful, or sparkly that people wear them in jewelry. The rarer the gem, the more it costs!

MOST EXPENSIVE

Diamonds form deep in the Earth and contain just one element: carbon. Pure diamonds are rare. Colored ones are even rarer and more expensive.

A pure diamond is colorless.

The element boron can turn a diamond blue. ▶

Costly gem

The most expensive gem is the Pink Star diamond. In 2017 it sold for more than $71 million!

SEEING RED

Rubies and garnets are eye-catching red gemstones. Rubies are crystals of the mineral corundum that have been tinted by the element chromium.

A ruby comes in different shades of red.

Garnets form in metamorphic rocks.

Finding
Fossils

Hunt for fossils where rocks are broken open or worn away. With an adult's help, search cliffs, quarries, and riverbeds.

WHAT ARE FOSSILS?

Fossils are the remains of ancient animals or plants. They form when a dead body or plant is covered in mud or sand before it rots. Over thousands of years, the mud or sand turns to rock, along with the hard parts of the animal or plant.

▲ These are fossils of ancient shelled sea creatures called ammonites.

FOSSILS IN ROCK

Sedimentary rocks such as sandstone, limestone, and mudstone are good for fossil-hunting. They contain fossils of bones, shells, and bark.

The bones of this fish were preserved in sandstone.

DINOSAUR DAYS

Scientists piece together fossil bones to build whole skeletons. Thanks to fossils, we know what dinosaurs looked like, even though they died out millions of years ago.

Fossil giants

The biggest fossils belong to giant plant-eating dinosaurs.

Pterodactylus was a winged reptile that lived in dinosaur times.

Glossary

atom The tiniest part of an element that can exist by itself.

core The center of a planet.

crystal The regular shape that a mineral forms as it grows.

dinosaur One of a group of reptiles that lived on land from 230 to 66 million years ago.

dissolve Mixes in with water or another liquid.

earthquake Shaking of the ground caused by movements of the plates of rock that form Earth's surface.

element A pure, basic substance.

erosion Wearing away by wind, water, or ice.

evaporate Change from a liquid into a gas, for example when water boils it evaporates as steam.

fossil The remains of an animal or plant that lived long ago, pressed into rock or turned into rock.

fuel A material that is burned to make heat or power.

gemstone A mineral or rock that is valued for its strength and beauty.

igneous rock Rock formed when magma cools and hardens.

lava Magma that has spilled onto the Earth's surface.

magma Hot, runny rock beneath the Earth's surface of cool, hardened rock.

metal A solid that is usually hard and shiny. Metal melts when it is heated and can also be hammered into new shapes.

metamorphic rock Rock formed when any rock is changed by enormous heat or pressure.

mineral A solid formed in the ground or in water.

ore A mineral or rock that contains large amounts of a metal.

plate One of the giant slabs of rock that make up the surface of the Earth.

quarry A place where rocks or minerals are dug from the ground.

rarer Found less often.

rock A solid made from different minerals.

sedimentary rock Rock formed when sand, mud, minerals, or plants and animal remains are pressed together until they harden.

solid With a fixed shape; a solid is not a liquid or a gas.

stalactite A column of dangling rock, formed by dripping water containing minerals.

stalagmite A column of rock growing up from the floor of a cave.

volcano A hole in the Earth's crust through which lava, gas, and ash can erupt.

Index

PICTURE CREDITS

Alamy: 7br (World History Archive/NASA), 9br (Natural History Museum, London), 13br (mauritius images GmbH/Raimund Linke), 19cr (Sotheby's Auction House, London/Jack Taylor); **Getty Images:** front cover (Daniel Viñé Garcia); **Shutterstock:** back cover (Sebastian Janicki), 1 (vvoe), 2-3 (Zuieva Oleksandra), 4lt (Tyler Boyes), 4lc (michal812), 4bl (Zelenskaya), 4c (fotosaga), 4bc (Tyler Boyes), 4-5 (MH Anderson Photography), 5t (Prafatsum), 5r (NigelSpiers), 6 (leungchopan), 6b (Rainer Albiez), 7t (Roserunn), 7bl (Grigory Ignatev), 8-9 (pisaphotography), 9tl (kikujungboy), 9cr (Sinelev), 10 (Waj), 11t (holbox), 11b (Julien Hautcoeur), 11br (Lidiya Oleandra), 12-13 (noreefly), 12br (N8Allen), 13tr (Zack Frank), 14bl (Albert Russ), 14br (Cagla Acikgoz), 15tr (Jiri Vaclavek), 15bl (Bambuh), 15br (Sebastian Janicki), 16 (Mark Agnor), 17t (Djelen), 17b (frank_peters), 17cr (Fokin Oleg), 18l (royaltystockphoto), 18-19b (Sararwut Jaimassiri), 18-19t (NickKnight), 19br (vvoe), 20-21 (YuRi Photolife), 20br (sarkao), 21tr (Mike Truchon), 21br (David Roland).